THE RAPTURE

Thomas Ice and Timothy Demy

HARVEST HOUSE PUBLISHERS
Eugene, Oregon 97402

THE TRUTH ABOUT THE RAPTURE

Copyright © 1996 by Pre-Trib Research Center
Published by Harvest House Publishers
Eugene, Oregon 97402

ISBN 1-56507-392-4

Printed in the United States of America.

97   98   99   00   01   02   —   10   9   8   7   6   5   4   3

Contents

P A R T   4

What Is the Significance
of the Pretribulational Rapture
for the Believer Today?

POCKET PROPHECY SERIES

About this series...

The Pocket Prophecy Series is designed to provide readers a brief summary of individual topics and issues in Bible prophecy. So that they might be used for quick reference or during short periods of time, the works are written in a question-and-answer format. The questions follow a logical progression so that those reading straight through will receive a greater appreciation for the topic and the issues involved. Each issue is fully documented and contains a bibliography of recommended reading for those who desire to pursue their study in greater depth.

The theological perspective presented throughout the series is that of premillennialism and pretribulationism. The authors recognize that this is not the only position embraced by evangelical Christians, but we believe that it is the most widely held and prominent perspective. It is also our conviction that premillennialism and, specifically, pretribulationism, best explains the prophetic plan of God as revealed in the Bible.

The study of prophecy and its puzzling pieces is an endeavor which is detailed and complex, but not beyond comprehension or resolution. It is open to error, misinterpretation, and confusion. Such possibilities should not, however, cause any Christian to shy away from either the study of prophecy or engagement in honest and helpful discussions about it. The goal of this series is to provide all those who desire to better understand the Scriptures with a concise and consistent tool. If you will do the digging, the rewards will be great and the satisfaction will remain with you as you grow in your knowledge and love of our Lord Jesus Christ and His Word.

P A R T   1

Introduction to the Pretribulational Rapture

1. What is the pretribulational rapture?

A recent survey by *U.S. News & World Report* found that 61 percent of Americans believe that Jesus Christ will return to earth, and 44 percent believe in the rapture of the church.[1] What is the rapture? With so much popular certainty, why is there so much interpretative confusion over these events? The doctrine of the pretribulational rapture is an important biblical teaching not only because it provides insights into the future, but also because it provides Christians with motivation for contemporary living.

The pretribulational rapture teaches that, prior to the seven-year tribulation, all members of the body of Christ (both living and dead) will be caught up in the air to meet Christ and then be taken to heaven.

The teaching of the rapture is most clearly presented in 1 Thessalonians 4:13-18. In this passage Paul informs his readers that living Christians at the time of the rapture will be reunited with those who have died in Christ before them. In verse 17 the English phrase "caught up" translates the Greek word *harpazó*, which means "to seize upon with force" or "to snatch up." This word is used 14 times in the Greek New Testament in a variety of ways.

Sometimes the New Testament uses *harpazó* with the sense of "stealing," "carrying off," or "dragging away" (Matthew 12:29; John 10:12). It also can have the meaning of "to lead away forcibly" (John 6:15; 10:28,29; Acts 23:10; Jude 23). However, for our purposes, a third usage is significant. This usage is that of God's Spirit carrying someone away. We see this usage four times (Acts 8:39; 2 Corinthians 12:2,4; 1 Thessalonians 4:17; Revelations 12:5).[2]

This latter usage is illustrated in Acts 8:39 where Philip, upon completion of the baptism of the Ethiopian eunuch, is "caught up" and divinely transported from the desert to the coastal town of Azotus. Similarly, the church will, in a moment of time, be taken from earth to heaven. It is not surprising that one contemporary author has called this unique event "The Great Snatch."

Some critics have noted that the word *rapture* is never used in the Bible. While this is true of English versions, Latin translators of the Greek New Testament *did* use the word *rapere*, which is the root of the English term *rapture*. Many contemporary theological terms have been derived from a Latin base. Throughout much of the history of the Western church, Latin was the accepted language of theological discussion. As a result, many theological terms developed out of this language (i.e., Trinity). Our current term *rapture* is also such a term. As will be seen in the answer to the next question, there are many terms used in the New Testament to refer to the rapture event. Thus, to claim that the rapture should be dismissed on the grounds of language is naively incorrect.

2. What terms does the New Testament use when referring to the rapture?

The New Testament uses a variety of terms to describe the multifaceted aspects of the rapture.

- *harpazó*—"caught up," "to seize upon with force," "to snatch up."
  "Then we who are alive and remain shall be *caught up* together with them in the clouds to meet the Lord in the air, and thus we shall always be with the Lord" (1 Thessalonians 4:17).

- *episunagógé*—"gathering together," "assembly."
  "Now we request you, brethren, with regard to the coming of our Lord Jesus Christ and our *gathering together* to Him" (2 Thessalonians 2:1).

- *allassó*—"to change," "to transform," "to exchange."
  "Behold, I tell you a mystery; we shall not all sleep, but we shall all be *changed*, in a moment, in the twinkling

of an eye, at the last trumpet; for the trumpet will sound, and the dead will be raised imperishable, and we shall be *changed*" (1 Corinthians 15:51,52).

- *paralambanó*—"to take to," "to receive to oneself." "If I go and prepare a place for you, I will come again, and *receive* you to Myself, that where I am, there you may be also" (John 14:3).

- *epiphaneia*—"a manifestation," "an appearance." "... looking for the blessed hope and *the appearing* of the glory of our great God and Savior, Christ Jesus" (Titus 2:13).

- *rhuomai*—"to draw to oneself," "to rescue," "to deliver." "... and to wait for His Son from heaven, whom He raised from the dead, that is Jesus, who *delivers* us from the wrath to come" (1 Thessalonians 1:10).

- *apokalupsis*—"an uncovering," "laying bare," "a revealing, revelation." "Therefore, gird your minds for action, keep sober in spirit, fix your hope completely on the grace to be brought to you at *the revelation* of Jesus Christ" (1 Peter 1:13).

- *parousia*—"a being present, presence," "a coming," "an arrival." "Be patient, therefore, brethren, until *the coming* of the Lord. Behold, the farmer waits for the precious produce of the soil, being patient about it, until it gets the early and late rains. You too be patient; strengthen your hearts, for *the coming* of the Lord is at hand" (James 5:7,8).

Not every use of these words in the New Testament is a rapture reference. The context determines the meaning.

3. What do these terms teach concerning the nature of the rapture?

A review of these terms teaches that the rapture will be an event initiated by Christ in which He comes in the clouds and appears to believers. His revelation will result in drawing, gathering, catching up, and receiving to Himself those same believers. During this event, Christians of all time will be transformed; the living will be translated apart from death, while those asleep in Christ will be resurrected. All these will then accompany the Son to the Father's heavenly house which has been prepared for them.

4. When does the rapture take place in relation to the tribulation?

There are five major views within premillennialism concerning the timing of the rapture in relation to the seven-year tribulation.

- *Pretribulationism*—This view teaches that all Christians will be taken in the rapture which will occur before the tribulation.

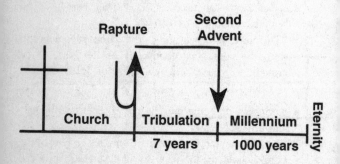

- *Partial rapture*—This view teaches that the rapture occurs before the tribulation, but only "spiritual" Christians will be taken, while other Christians will remain through the tribulation.

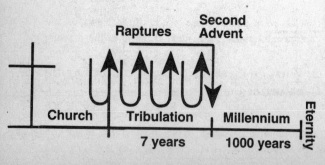

- *Midtribulationism*—This view teaches that all Christian will be taken in the rapture in the middle (after the first 3¹/₂ years) of the tribulation.

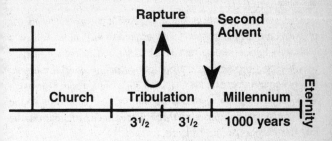

Pre-wrath rapture—This view teaches that all Christians will be taken in the rapture approximately three-fourths of the way through the tribulation.

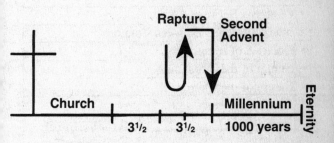

- *Posttribulationism*—This view teaches that all Christians will be raptured at the end of the tribulation.

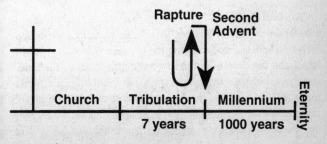

There are many arguments for and against each of the views above, and it is our hope to deal with such issues in future books in this series. However, the purpose of this work is to set forth a positive presentation of pretribulationism. It is to this task that we now turn.

It is our desire in this book to provide an *overview* of the pretribulational perspective. Our approach will be to follow a biblically logical order. Just as a builder constructs a house by first laying a proper foundation upon which to build the house, so also sound doctrine rests upon a sure foundation. Our overview of pretribulationism can be summarized according to the following chart composed of three elements: the foundation, the body of the house, and the roof.

Practical Motivation for Godly Living		
Pretrib Rapture		
• Contrasts Between Comings		
• Interval Needed Between Comings		
• Doctrine of Imminency		
• Nature of the Tribulation		
• Nature of the Church		
• Work of the Holy Spirit		
Premillen-nialism	Futurism	Israel/Church Distinction
Consistent Literal Interpretation		

The four elements of the biblical *foundation* supporting pretribulationism are consistent literal interpretation, premillennialism, futurism, and a distinction between God's program for Israel and the church. In the illustration, the *body of the house* represents six major arguments found in the Bible for pretribulationism. These are not the only reasons to believe in a pretrib rapture, but they encompass much of the evidence. The *roof* of the house represents the practical implications springing forth from a consistently applied pretribulationism.

P A R T   2

What Is the Biblical Foundation for the Pretribulational Rapture?

Many biblical doctrines cannot be properly understood apart from certain foundational truths. Four affirmations provide the biblical foundation for the pretribulational rapture: 1) *consistent* literal interpretation, 2) premillennialism, 3) futurism, and 4) a distinction between Israel and the church.

5. How should prophecy be interpreted?

Consistent literal interpretation is essential to properly understanding what God is saying in the Bible. Yet some people believe that consistent literal interpretation is either impossible or impractical. One critic believes it to be a "presumption" that "is unreasonable" and "an impossible ideal."[3] In spite of false characterization, what do we mean by consistent literal interpretation?

A Definition of Literal Interpretation

The dictionary defines *literal* as "belonging to letters." Further, it says literal interpretation involves an approach "based on the actual words in their ordinary meaning . . . not going beyond the facts."[4] "Literal interpretation of the Bible simply means to explain the original sense of the Bible according to the normal and customary usages of its language."[5] How is this done? It can only be accomplished through an interpretation of the written text which includes consideration of the grammatical (according to the rules of grammar), historical (consistent with the historical setting of the passage), contextual (in accord with its context) method of interpretation. This is what literalists mean by consistently literal interpretation.

Grammatical, Historical, Contextual Interpretation

Grammatical

The grammatical aspect of literal interpretation considers the impact that grammar plays on a passage. This means that a student of the text should correctly analyze the grammatical relationships of words, phrases, and sentences to one another. Dr. Roy Zuck writes:

> When we speak of interpreting the Bible grammatically, we are referring to the process of seeking to determine its meaning by ascertaining four things: (a) the meaning of words (lexicology), (b) the form of words (morphology), (c) the function of words (parts of speech), and (d) the relationships of words (syntax).[6]

Dr. Zuck gives further amplification of the four areas noted above:

> In the meaning of words (lexicology), we are concerned with (a) etymology—how words are derived and developed, (b) usage—how words are used by the same and other authors, (c) synonyms and antonyms—how similar and opposite words are used, and (d) context—how words are used in various contexts.
>
> In discussing the form of words (morphology) we are looking at how words are structured and how that affects their meaning. For example the word *eat* means something different from *ate*, though the same letters are used. The word *part* changes meaning when the letter *s* is added to it to make the word *parts*. The function of words (parts of speech) considers what the various forms do. These include attention to subjects, verbs, objects, nouns, and others. . . . The relationships of words (syntax) are the way words are related or put together to form phrases, clauses, and sentences.[7]

The grammatical aspect of literal interpretation lets us know that any interpretation conflicting with grammar is invalid.

Historical

Proper interpretation of the Bible means that the historical context must be taken into account. This aspect means that one must consider the historical setting and circumstances in which the books of the Bible were written. Dr. Paul Tan explains:

> The proper concept of the historical in Bible interpretation is to view the Scriptures as written during given ages

and cultures. Applications may then be drawn which are relevant to our times. For instance, the subject of meat offered to idols can only be interpreted from the historical and cultural setting of New Testament times. Principles to be drawn are relevant to us today.[8]

Contextual

"A passage taken out of context is a pretext." This slogan is certainly true! Yet, one of the most common mistakes made by those who are found to have misinterpreted a passage in the Bible is that of taking a verse out of its divinely ordered context. Even though a sentence may be taken from the Bible, it is not the Word of God if it is placed into a context which changes the meaning from that which God intended in its original context. Dr. Zuck writes:

> The context in which a given Scripture passage is written influences how that passage is to be understood. Context includes several things:
>
> - the verse(s) immediately before and after a passage
> - the paragraph and book in which the verses occur
> - the dispensation in which it was written
> - the message of the entire Bible
> - the historical-cultural environment of that time when it was written.[9]

A widely used example of a verse taken out of context is 2 Chronicles 7:14: "and My people who are called by My name humble themselves and pray...." Usually this is quoted as an explanation for why America is in decline. Because "My people" are addressed, it is said that the success of a nation is dependent upon the obedience of Christians to the Lord. Thus, God blesses or curses a nation in accordance with Christian obedience. Then 2 Chronicles 7:14 is cited as a formula for national restoration because the passage says to "humble themselves and pray, and seek My face and turn from their wicked ways, then I will hear from heaven, will forgive their sin, and will heal their land."

We believe that this is an illustration of a passage taken out of context because of the following contextual factors:

- "My people" is said in 2 Chronicles 6:24 to be "Israel," as is also indicated by the flow of the historical context.

- Solomon is preparing to dedicate the recently completed temple, and 7:14 is God's renewal of the Mosaic covenant under which Israel and only Israel operates.

Since this passage involves Israel and not the church, it is improper to speculatively relate it to present-day American Christianity. Proper contextual interpretation allows for the general observation that God delights in a humble and obedient people, but obedience and prayer should be offered according to His plan for the church.

Figures of Speech

Literal interpretation recognizes that a word or phrase can be used either plainly (denotative) or figuratively (connotative). As in our own conversations today, the Bible may use plain speech, such as "He died yesterday" (denotative use of language). Or the same thing may be said in a more colorful way: "He kicked the bucket yesterday" (connotative use of language). An important point to be noted is that even though we may use a figure of speech to refer to someone's death, we are using that figure to refer to an event that literally happened. Some interpreters mistakenly think that just because a figure of speech may be used to describe an event (i.e., Jonah's experience in the belly of the great fish in Jonah 2) that the event was not literal. Such is not the case. A "golden rule of interpretation" has been developed to help us discern whether or not a figure of speech was intended by an author:

> When the plain sense of Scripture makes common sense, seek no other sense; therefore, take every word at its primary, ordinary, usual, literal meaning unless the facts of the immediate context, studied in the light of related passages and axiomatic and fundamental truths, indicate clearly otherwise.[10]

Literalists understand that a figure of speech is employed by Isaiah teaching that the Adamic curse upon nature will be reversed in the millennium when he says, "And all the trees of the field will clap their hands" (Isaiah 55:12). This figure is discerned by specific factors in the context in which it was written, all dealing with the removal of the curse upon nature at this future time. Even though figurative language is employed, it will literally happen in history.

Literal Versus Literal

Dr. Elliott Johnson has noted that much of the confusion over literal interpretation can be removed when one properly understands the two primary ways the term has been used down through church history: "(1) the clear, plain sense of a word or phrase as over against a figurative use, and (2) a system that views the text as providing the basis of the true interpretation."[11] Thus, literalists by and large have used the term *literal* to refer to their system of interpretation (the consistent use of the grammatical-historical system (Johnson's second definition). And once inside that system, *literal* refers to whether or not a specific word or phrase is used in its context in a figurative or literal sense (Johnson's first definition).

Johnson's second use of literal (i.e., systematic literalism) is simply the grammatical-historical system consistently used. The grammatical-historical system was revived by the Reformers. It was set against the spiritual (spiritualized) or deeper meaning of the text that was a common approach during the Middle Ages. The literal meaning was used simply as a springboard to a deeper ("spiritual") meaning, which was viewed as more desirable. A classic spiritualized interpretation would, for example, see the four rivers of Genesis 2—the Pishon, Havilah, Tigris, and Euphrates—as representing the human body, soul, spirit, and mind. Coming from such a system, the Reformers saw the need to get back to the literal or textual meaning of the Bible. For instance, Martin Luther wanted to debate John Eck from the *text* of the Bible.

The system of literal interpretation is the grammatical-historical or textual approach to interpretation. Use of literalism in this sense could be called "macroliteralism." Within macro-literalism, the consistent use of the grammatical-historical system yields the interpretative conclusion, for example, that *Israel* always and only refers to national Israel. The church will not be substituted for Israel if the grammatical-historical system of interpretation is consistently used because there are no indicators in the text of Scripture that such is the case. Therefore, one must bring an idea from outside the text by saying that the passage really means something that it does not actually say. This kind of replacement approach is a mild form of spiritualized or allegorical interpretation. So it is true to speak of those who replace *Israel* with *the church* as not taking the Bible literally and spiritualizing the text, since such a belief is contrary to a macroliteral interpretation.

Consistent literal interpreters, within the framework of the grammatical-historical system, do discuss whether or not a word, phrase, or the literary genre of a biblical book is a figure of speech (connotative) or is to be taken literally/plainly (denotative). There is discussion among literalists as to whether or not a given word or phrase is being used as a figure of speech, based on the context of a given passage. Some passages are quite naturally clearer than others and a consensus among interpreters develops, whereas other passages may find literal interpreters divided as to whether or not these passages should be taken as figures of speech. However, this is more a problem of application than of method.

God's Word is to be understood through literal interpretation. It is an important foundation stone supporting the pretribulational rapture. When the Bible is consistently interpreted literally, from Genesis to Revelation, the pretribulational position is hard to avoid.

6. What is premillennialism?

The second foundation stone supporting the pretribulational rapture of the church is the biblical doctrine known as premillennialism. Premillennialism teaches that the second advent will occur before Christ's thousand-year reign from Jerusalem upon earth. In the early church, premillennialism was called *chiliasm*, from the Greek term meaning "1,000" used six times in Revelation 20:2-7. Dr. Charles Ryrie cites essential features of premillennialism as follows: "Its duration will be 1,000 years; its location will be on this earth; its government will be

PREMILLENNIALISM

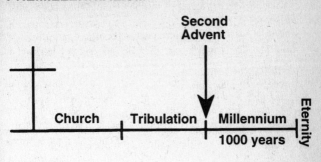

POSTMILLENNIALISM

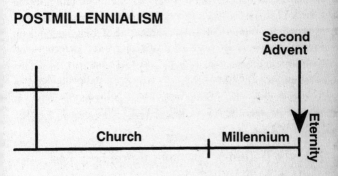

AMILLENNIALISM

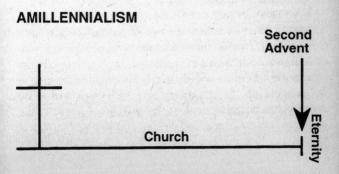

theocratic with the personal presence of Christ reigning as King; and it will fulfill all the yet-unfulfilled promises about the earthly kingdom."[12]

Premillennialism is contrasted with the postmillennial teaching that Christ will return after He has reigned spiritually from His throne in heaven for a long period of time during the current age, through the church, and the similar amillennial view that also advocates a present, but pessimistic, spiritual reign of Christ. Biblical premillennialism is a necessary foundation for pretribulationism since it is impossible for either postmillennialism or amillennialism to support pretribulationism.

Premillennialism is merely the result of interpreting the whole Bible, Genesis to Revelation, in the most natural way—literally. Many of the critics admit that if the literal approach is applied consistently to the whole of Scripture, then premillennialism is the natural result. If the Old Testament promises are ever going to be fulfilled literally for Israel as a nation, then they are yet in the future. This is also supportive of premillennialism. Premillennialism also provides a satisfactory and victorious end to history in time as man through Christ satisfactorily fulfills his creation mandate to rule over the world. Premillennialism is a necessary biblical prerequisite needed to build the later biblical doctrine of the rapture of the church before the seven-year tribulation.

7. Is the fulfillment of biblical prophecy past, present, or future?

We believe the answer to this question is "future." The third biblical foundation for a systematic understanding of the pretribulation rapture is futurism. An important, but seemingly little-recognized aspect of proper interpretation of Bible prophecy is the role of timing. When will a prophecy be fulfilled in history? There are four possibilities. The four views are simple in the sense that they reflect the only four possibilities in relation to time: past, present, future, and timeless.

The *preterist* (past) believes that most, if not all prophecy has already been fulfilled, usually in relation to the destruction of Jerusalem in A.D. 70. The *historicist* (present) sees much of the current church age as equal to the tribulation period. Thus, prophecy has been and will be fulfilled during the current church age. *Futurists* (future) believe that virtually all prophetic events will not occur in the current church age, but will take place in the future tribulation, second coming, or millennium. The *idealist* (timeless) does not believe either that the Bible indicates the timing of events or that we can determine their timing in advance. Therefore, idealists think that prophetic passages mainly teach great ideas or truths about God to be applied regardless of timing.

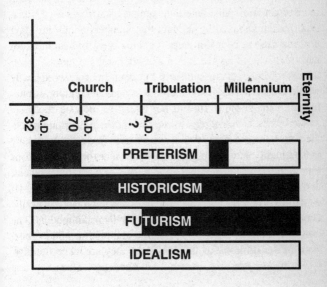

The Significance of Futurism

Of the four views noted above, the only one that logically and historically has supported the pretribulational position is futurism. Why? Because the timing of the rapture relates to when the tribulation will occur in history. Preterism declares that the tribulation has already taken place. Historicism says that the tribulation started in the fourth century with events surrounding Constantine's Christianization of the Roman Empire and continues until the second coming. Idealism denies that there is a timing of events. Thus, only futurism, which sees the tribulation as a yet future event, could even allow for a rapture before the beginning of that seven-year period. This does not mean, however, that all futurists are pretribulationists; they are not. *But to be a pretribulationist, one must be a futurist.*

Support for Futurism

A defense of futurism can be developed from the Bible by comparing and contrasting futurism with the other three approaches. For example, *futurism instead of preterism* can be shown by demonstrating from specific texts of Scripture that "coming" in the debated passages refers to a bodily return of Christ to planet Earth, not a mystical coming mediated through the Roman army. One area that supports *futurism over historicism* is demonstrated by the fact that numbers relating to days and years are to be taken literally. There is no biblical basis for days really meaning years. A major argument for *futurism over idealism* is the fact that numbers do count. In other words, why would God give hundreds of chronological and temporal statements in the Bible if He did not intend to indicate such?

Let's look at some general support for the futurist approach. First and foremost, only the futurist can interpret the whole Bible literally and, having done so, harmonize those conclusions into a consistent theological system. Just as the people, places, and times were meant to be understood literally in Genesis 1–11, so the texts that relate to the end times are to be taken literally. Days mean days; years mean years; months mean months. The only way that the book of Revelation and other prophetic portions of the Bible make any sense is if they are taken literally, which means that they have not yet happened. Thus, they are future.

The Bible is one-third prophecy, and the majority of that is yet unfulfilled prophecy. Since a consistently literal approach to the whole Bible (including prophecy) is the proper way of understanding God's revelation to man, the futurist approach is the correct way of looking at the timing of biblical prophecy. Only the futurist understanding of biblical prophecy can support the pretribulational rapture.

8. What is the relationship between Israel and the church in prophecy?

"The New Testament consistently differentiates between Israel and the church," claims Dr. Arnold Fruchtenbaum.[13] Fruchtenbaum supports this conclusion through a powerful two-fold argument in which he first demonstrates the biblical view of Israel and then shows that the church is viewed in the New Testament as a separate entity.

*The Distinction Between
Israel and the Church*

The fourth biblical foundation upon which the pretrib rapture is built is the fact that God has two peoples: Israel and the church. What do we mean by this distinction, and how does it impact pretribulationism?

Belief that God's single plan for history includes the two peoples of Israel and the church does not imply that there are thus different ways of salvation. When it comes to the issue of salvation, there is only one way since all people down through history descend from a single source: Adam. Christ's saving work is the only way of salvation for anyone, whether the person is a member of Israel or the church.

Israel

Fruchtenbaum notes that "the term *Israel* is viewed theologically as referring to all descendants of Abraham, Isaac, and Jacob, also known as Jews, the Jewish people, Israelites, Hebrews, etc."[14] He notes that national election distinguishes Israel from those peoples who were not chosen (that we know as Gentiles), and he outlines four reasons for Israel's election: 1) They were "chosen on the basis of God's love...to be 'a kingdom of priests and a holy nation' (Ex. 19:6)...to represent the Gentile nations before God." 2) "God chose Israel to be the recipient of His revelation and to record it (Deut. 4:5-8; 6:6-9; Rom. 3:1-2)." 3) Israel "was to propagate the doctrine of the One God (Deut. 6:4)." 4) Israel "was to produce the Messiah (Rom. 9:5; Heb. 2:16-17; 7:13-14)."[15]

No biblically oriented Christian would deny these purposes relating to Israel. The differences begin to emerge when we consider Israel in relation to the church. "Some theologians insist," notes Fruchtenbaum "that at some point the church receives the promises given to Israel and thus becomes the 'New Israel' (known as replacement theology). Some believe the terms *church* and *Israel* are used virtually 'interchangeably,' most citing Galatians 6:16 and some Romans 9:6."[16]

However, people commonly known as dispensationalists interpret the Bible literally and thus do not confuse the terms *Israel* and *the church*, since there is no basis in the text of any biblical passage for supporting such an approach.

Having noted important aspects of the biblical use of *Israel,* we will now examine the nature of the church.

The Church

Six reasons are given by Fruchtenbaum from the Bible supporting the notion that the church is a distinct work in God's household from His people Israel.

1. "The first evidence is the fact that *the church was born at Pentecost*, whereas Israel had existed for many centuries."[17] This, supported by "the use of the future tense in Matthew 16:18, shows that it did not exist in gospel history."[18] The church, born at Pentecost, is called the body of Christ (Colossians 1:18). Entrance into the body is through Spirit baptism (1 Corinthians 12:13), in which Jew and Gentile are united. It is evident that the church began on the day of Pentecost since Acts 1:5 views Spirit baptism as future, while Acts 10 links it to the past, specifically to Pentecost.

2. "The second evidence is that *certain events in the ministry of the Messiah were essential to the establishment of the church*—the church does not come into being until certain events have taken place."[19] These events include the resurrection and ascension of Jesus to become head of the church (Ephesians 1:20-23). "The church, with believers as the body and Christ as the head, did not exist until after Christ ascended to become its head. And it could not become a functioning entity until after the Holy Spirit provided the necessary spiritual gifts (Ephesians 4:7-11)."[20]

3. "The third evidence is *the mystery character of the church*."[21] A mystery in the Bible is a hidden truth not revealed until the New Testament (Ephesians 3:3-5,9; Colossians 1:26,27). Fruchtenbaum lists "four defining characteristics of the church [that] are described as a mystery. (1) The body concept of Jewish and Gentile believers united into one body is designated as a mystery in Ephesians 3:1-12. (2) The doctrine of Christ indwelling every believer, the Christ-in-you concept, is called a mystery in Colossians 1:24-27 (cf. Colossians 2:10-19; 3:4). (3) The church as the Bride of Christ is called a mystery in Ephesians 5:22-32. (4) The Rapture is called a mystery in 1 Corinthians 15:50-58. These four mysteries describe qualities that distinguish the church from Israel."[22]

4. "The fourth evidence that the church is distinct from Israel is the *unique relationship between Jews and the Gentiles*, called one new man in Ephesians 2:15."[23] During the current church age God is saving a remnant from the two previous entities (Israel and Gentiles) and combining them into a third

new object—the church. This unity of Jews and Gentiles into one new man covers only the church age, from Pentecost until the rapture, after which time God will restore Israel and complete her destiny (Acts 15:14-18). First Corinthians 10:32 reflects just such a division when it says, "Give no offense either to Jews or to Greeks or to the church of God."

5. "The fifth evidence for the distinction between Israel and the church is found in Galatians 6:16."[24] "It appears logical to view 'the Israel of God' (Galatians 6:16) as believing Jews in contrast to unbelieving Jews called 'Israel after the flesh' (1 Corinthians 10:18)."[25] This passage does not support the false claim of replacement theologians who claim that Israel is supplanted by the church. Instead, the Bible teaches that a remnant of Israel is combined with elect Gentiles during this age to make up a whole new entity the New Testament calls the church (Ephesians 2).

Replacement theology tries to teach that because Gentile believers are described as "Abraham's offspring," (Galatians 3:29) this is equivalent to saying that they are Israel. This is clearly not the case. Paul's description of Gentile believers in Galatians 3:29 simply means that they participate in the spiritual (i.e., salvation) blessings that come through Israel (Romans 15:27; 1 Corinthians 9:11,14). "Those who are the spiritual seed are partakers of Jewish spiritual blessings but are never said to become partakers of the physical, material, or national promises."[26] Therefore, Israel's national promises are left intact, awaiting a yet future fulfillment.

6. "In the book of Acts, both Israel and the church exist simultaneously. *The term Israel is used twenty times and* ekklesia *(church) nineteen times, yet the two groups are always kept distinct.*"[27] Thus, the replacement theologian has no actual biblical basis upon which he bases his theological claim that Israel and the church have become one.

The Significance of the Distinction

If Israel and the church are not distinguished, then there is no basis for seeing a future for Israel or for the church as a new and unique people of God. If Israel and the church are merged into a single program, then the Old Testament promises for Israel will never be fulfilled and are usually seen by replacement theologians as spiritually fulfilled by the church. The merging of

Israel's destiny into the church not only makes into one what the Scriptures understand as two, but it also removes a need for future restoration of God's original elect people in order to fulfill literally His promise that they will one day be the head and not the tail (Deuteronomy 28:13).

The more that believers see a distinct plan for Israel and a distinct plan for the church, the more they realize that when the New Testament speaks to the church it is describing a separate destiny and hope for her. The church becomes more distinct in the plan of God. Israel's future includes the seven-year tribulation, and then shortly before Christ's return to Jerusalem she will be converted to Jesus as her Messiah as the veil is removed and she looks upon the one who was pierced. On the other hand, the distinct hope (the rapture before the seventieth week of Daniel) for the church is Christ's any-moment return.

Thus, a distinction between Israel and the church, as taught in the Bible, provides a basis of support for the pretribulational rapture. Those who merge the two programs cannot logically support the biblical arguments for pretribulationism.

P A R T   3

What Are the Biblical Evidences for the Pretribulational Rapture?

9. Why are the rapture and the second coming separate events?

In the previous section we gave a basis or foundation for pretribulationism. In this section we will begin laying out specific biblical evidence for the pretribulational rapture. The first place to start is with the biblical notion that the rapture of the church is distinct from Christ's second coming to the earth.

John Feinberg notes that distinguishing between the rapture and second coming is important in establishing pretribulationism against the non-pretribulational claim that the Bible does not teach such a view:

> The pretribulationist must show that there is enough dissimilarity between clear rapture and clear second advent passages as to warrant the claim that the two kinds

of passages *could* be speaking about two events which *could* occur at different times. The pretribulationist does not have to prove at this point . . . that the two events must occur at different times, but only that the exegetical data from rapture and second advent passages do not make it impossible for the events to occur at different times. If he can do that, the pretribulationist has shown that his view is not impossible. And, he has answered the posttribulationist's strongest line of evidence.[28]

A key factor in understanding the New Testament's teaching of the pretribulational rapture revolves around the fact that two future comings of Christ are presented. The first coming is the catching up into the clouds of the church before the seven-year tribulation and the second coming occurs at the end of the tribulation when Christ returns to the earth to begin His 1000-year kingdom. Anyone desirous of insight into the biblical teaching of the rapture and second advent must study and decide whether Scripture speaks of one or two future events.

Framing the Issue

Posttribulationists usually contend that if the rapture and the second coming are two distinct events, separated by about seven years, then there ought to be at least one passage in Scripture which clearly teaches this. However, the Bible does not always teach God's truth in accordance with our preconceived notions or in such a way that answers directly all of our questions. For example, a Unitarian could design a similar kind of question regarding the Trinity. "Where is at least one passage in Scripture which clearly says that the Persons of the Godhead are distinct?" We who believe the Trinity reply that the Bible teaches the Trinity but in a different way.

Many important biblical doctrines are not given to us directly from a single verse; we often need to harmonize passages into systematic conclusions. Some truths are directly stated in the Bible, such as the deity of Christ (John 1:1; Titus 2:13). But doctrines like the Trinity and the incarnate nature of Christ are the product of biblical harmonization. Taking into account all biblical texts, orthodox theologians over time recognized that God is a Trinity and that Christ is the God-Man. Similarly, a systematic consideration of all biblical passages reveals that Scripture teaches two future comings.

Posttribulationists often contend that the pretribulational position is built merely upon an assumption that certain verses "make sense" if and only if the pretribulational model of the rapture is assumed to be correct. However, they often fail to make it clear to their readers that posttribulationism is just as dependent upon assumptions. The error of posttribulationists stems from failure to observe actual biblical distinctions.

For example, Christ's ministry has two phases which revolve around His two comings. Phase one took place at Christ's first coming when He came in humiliation to suffer. Phase two will begin at Christ's second coming when He will reign on earth in power and glory. Failure to distinguish these two phases was a key factor in Israel's rejection of Jesus as Messiah at His first coming. In the same way, failure to see clear distinctions between the rapture and second advent leads many people to a misinterpretation of God's future plan.

The Nature of the Rapture

The rapture is most clearly presented in 1 Thessalonians 4:13-18. It is characterized in the Bible as a "translation coming" (1 Corinthians 15:51,52; 1 Thessalonians 4:15-17) in which Christ comes *for* His church. The second advent is Christ returning *with* His saints, descending from heaven to establish His earthly kingdom (Zechariah 14:4,5; Matthew 24:27-31). Dr. Ed Hindson observes:

> The rapture (or "translation") of the church is often paralleled to the "raptures" of Enoch (Genesis 5:24) and Elijah (2 Kings 2:12). In each case, the individual disappeared or was caught up into heaven. At His ascension, our Lord Himself was "taken up" into heaven (Acts 1:9). The biblical description of the rapture involves both the resurrection of deceased believers and the translation of living believers into the air to meet the Lord (1 Thessalonians 4:16-17; 1 Corinthians 15:51,52).[29]

Differences between the two events are harmonized naturally by the pretribulational position, while other views are not able to account comfortably for such distinctions. Notice the following chart that gives passages for the rapture and the second coming.

Rapture and Second Coming Passages

Rapture   **Second Advent**

"Seventieth Week"

Seven-Year Tribulation Period

Rapture Passages

John 14:1-3
Romans 8:19
1 Corinthians 1:7-8
1 Corinthians 15:51-53
1 Corinthians 16:22
Philippians 3:20,1
Philippians 4:5
Colossians 3:4
1 Thessalonians 1:10
1 Thessalonians 2:19
1 Thessalonians 4:13-18
1 Thessalonians 5:9
1 Thessalonians 5:23
2 Thessalonians 2:1
2 Thessalonians 2:3 (?)
1 Timothy 6:14
2 Timothy 4:1
2 Timothy 4:8
Titus 2:13
Hebrews 9:28
James 5:7-9
1 Peter 1:7,13
1 Peter 5:4
1 John 2:28-3:2
Jude 21
Revelation 2:25
Revelation 3:10
" 4:10

2nd Coming Passages

Daniel 2:44-45
Daniel 7:9-14
Daniel 12:1-3
Zechariah 12:10
Zechariah 14:1-15
Matthew 13:41
Matthew 24:15-31
Matthew 26:64
Mark 13:14-27
Mark 14:62
Luke 21:25-28
Acts 1:9-11
Acts 3:19-21
1 Thessalonians 3:13
2 Thessalonians 1:6-10
2 Thessalonians 2:8
1 Peter 4:12,13
2 Peter 3:1-14
Jude 14,15
Revelation 1:7
Revelation 19:11-20:6
Revelation 22:7,12,20

Rapture and Second Coming Contrasts

Rapture/Translation	Second Coming Established Kingdom
1. Translation of all believers	1. No translation at all
2. Translated saints go to heaven	2. Translated saints return to earth
3. Earth not judged	3. Earth judged and righteousness established
4. Imminent, any-moment, signless	4. Follows definite predicted signs, including tribulation
5. Not in the Old Testament	5. Predicted often in Old Testament
6. Believers only	6. Affects all men
7. Before the day of wrath	7. Concluding the day of wrath
8. No reference to Satan	8. Satan bound
9. Christ comes *for* His own	9. Christ comes *with* His own
10. He comes in the *air*	10. He comes to the *earth*
11. He claims His bride	11. He comes with His bride
12. Only His own see Him	12. Every eye shall see Him
13. Tribulation begins	13. Millennial kingdom begins

Dr. John Walvoord concludes that these "contrasts should make it evident that the translation of the church is an event quite different in character and time from the return of the Lord to establish His kingdom, and confirms the conclusion that the translation takes place before the tribulation."[30]

Additional Differences

Paul speaks of the rapture as a "mystery" (1 Corinthians 15:51-54)—that is, a truth not revealed until its disclosure by the apostles (Colossians 1:26), making it a separate event, while the second coming was predicted in the Old Testament (Daniel 12:1-3; Zechariah 12:10; 14:4).

The movement for the believer at the rapture is from earth to heaven, while it is from heaven to earth at the second advent. At the rapture the Lord comes *for* his saints (1 Thessalonians 4:16), while at the second coming the Lord comes *with* His saints (1 Thessalonians 3:13). At the rapture the Lord comes only for believers, but His return to the earth will impact all people. The rapture is a translation/resurrection event where the Lord takes believers to the Father's house in heaven (John 14:3), while at the second coming, believers return from heaven to the earth (Matthew 24:30). Hindson says, "The different aspects of our Lord's return are clearly delineated in the scriptures themselves.

The only real issue in the eschatological debate is the time *interval* between them."[31]

The Scriptures concerning Christ's coming in the air to rapture His church are too distinct to be reduced into a single coming at the end of the tribulation. These biblical distinctions provide a strong basis for the pretribulational rapture.

10. Why is an interval necessary between the two comings?

An interval or gap of time is needed between the rapture and the second coming in order to facilitate many events predicted in the Bible in a timely manner. Numerous items in the New Testament can be harmonized by a pretrib time gap of at least seven years, while proponents of other views, especially posttribulationists, are forced to postulate scenarios that would not realistically allow for normal passage of time. The following events are best temporally harmonized with an interval of time as put forth by pretribulationism.[32]

- Second Corinthians 5:10 teaches that all believers of this age must appear before the judgment seat of Christ in heaven. This event, often known as the "bema judgment" from the Greek word *bema*, is an event never mentioned in the detailed accounts connected with the second coming of Christ to the earth. Since such an evaluation would require some passage of time, the pretrib gap of seven years nicely accounts for such a requirement.

- Revelation 19:7-10 pictures the church as a bride who has been made ready for marriage (with "fine linen," which represents "the righteous acts of the saints") to her groom (Christ). The bride has already been clothed in preparation for her return at the second coming with Christ to the earth (Revelation 19:11-18). It follows that the church would already have to be complete and in heaven (because of the pretrib rapture) in order to have been prepared in the way that Revelation 19 describes. This requires an interval of time which pretribulationism handles well.

- The 24 elders of Revelation 4:1–5:14 are best understood as representatives of the church. Dr. Charles Ryrie explains:

In the New Testament, elders as the highest officials in the church do represent the whole church (cf. Acts 15:6; 20:28), and in the Old Testament, twenty-four elders were appointed by King David to represent the entire Levitical priesthood (1 Chronicles 24). When those twenty-four elders met together in the temple precincts in Jerusalem, the entire priestly house was represented. Thus it seems more likely that the elders represent redeemed human beings. . . . the church is included and is thus in heaven before the tribulation begins.[33]

If they refer to the church, then this would necessitate the rapture and reward of the church before the tribulation and would require a chronological gap for them to perform their heavenly duties during the seven-year tribulation.

- Believers who come to faith in Christ during the tribulation are not translated at Christ's second advent but carry on ordinary occupations such as farming and building houses, and they will bear children (Isaiah 65:20-25). This would be impossible if all saints were translated at the second coming to the earth, as posttribulationists teach. Because pretribulationists have at least a seven-year interval between the removal of the church at the rapture and the return of Christ to the earth, this is not a problem because many people will be saved during the interval and thus be available to populate the millennium in their natural bodies in order to fulfill Scripture.

- It would be impossible for the judgment of the Gentiles to take place after the second coming if the rapture and second coming are not separated by a gap of time. How would both saved and unsaved, still in their natural bodies, be separated in judgment if all living believers are translated at the second coming? This would be impossible if the translation takes place at the second coming, but it is solved through a pretribulational time gap.

- Dr. John F. Walvoord points out that if "the translation took place in connection with the second coming to the earth, there would be no need of separating the sheep from the goats at a subsequent judgment, but the separation would have taken place in the very act of the translation of the believers before Christ actually sets up His throne on earth (Matthew 25:31)."[34] Once again, such a "problem" is solved by taking a pretrib position with its gap of at least seven years.

- A time interval is needed so that God's program for the church, a time when Jew and Gentile are united in one body (cf. Ephesians 2–3), will not become commingled in any way with His unfinished and future plan for Israel during the tribulation. Dr. Renald Showers notes:

   All other views of the Rapture have the church going through at least part of the 70th week, meaning that all other views mix God's 70-weeks program for Israel and Jerusalem together with His program for the church.[35]

   A gap is needed in order for these two aspects of God's program to be harmonized in a nonconflicting manner.

The pretribulational rapture of the church not only allows for the biblical distinction between the translation of church-age saints at the rapture and the second coming, but it also handles without difficulty the necessity of a time gap which harmonizes a number of future biblical events. This requirement of a seven-year gap of time adds support to the likelihood that pretribulationism best reflects the biblical viewpoint.

11. Why is imminency significant for the rapture?

The New Testament teaching that Christ could return and rapture His church at any moment, without prior signs or warning (i.e., imminency), is such a powerful argument for pretribulationism that it is one of the most fiercely attacked doctrines by pretrib opponents. Non-pretribulationists sense that if the New Testament teaches imminency, then a pretrib rapture is virtually assured.

What is a definition of *imminency*? Dr. Showers defines and describes *imminency* as follows:

1) An imminent event is one which is always "hanging overhead, is constantly ready to befall or overtake one; close at hand in its incidence." ("imminent," *The Oxford English Dictionary*, 1901, V, 66.) Thus, imminence carries the sense that it could happen at any moment. Other things *may* happen before the imminent event, but nothing else *must* take place before it happens. If something else must take place before an event can happen, then that event is not imminent. In other words, the necessity of something else taking place first destroys the concept of imminency.

2) Since a person never knows exactly when an imminent event will take place, then he cannot count on a certain amount of time transpiring before the imminent event happens. In light of this, he should always be prepared for it to happen at any moment.

3) A person cannot legitimately set or imply a date for its happening. As soon as a person sets a date for an imminent event he destroys the concept of imminency, because he thereby is saying that a certain amount of time must transpire before that event can happen. A specific date for an event is contrary to the concept that the event could happen at any moment.

4) A person cannot legitimately say that an imminent event will happen soon. The term "soon" implies that an event *must* take place "within a short time (after a particular point of time specified or implied)." By contrast, an imminent event *may* take place within a short time, but it does not *have* to do so in order to be imminent. As I hope you can see by now, "imminent" is not equal to "soon."[36]

The fact that Christ could return soon, at any moment (but may not) is a support for pretribulationism. What New Testament passages teach this truth? Those verses stating that Christ could return at any moment, without warning, and those instructing believers to wait and look for the Lord's coming include:

- *1 Corinthians 1:7*—"awaiting eagerly the revelation of our Lord Jesus Christ."

- *1 Corinthians 16:22*—"Maranatha."

- *Philippians 3:20*—"For our citizenship is in heaven, from which also we eagerly wait for a Savior, the Lord Jesus Christ."

- *Philippians 4:5*—"The Lord is near."

- *1 Thessalonians 1:10*—"to wait for His Son from heaven."

- *Titus 2:13*—"looking for the blessed hope and the appearing of the glory of our great God and Savior, Christ Jesus."

- *Hebrews 9:28*—"so Christ…shall appear a second time for salvation without reference to sin, to those who eagerly await Him."

- *James 5:7-9*—"Be patient, therefore, brethren, until the coming of the Lord…for the coming of the Lord is at hand.…Behold, the Judge is standing right at the door."

- *1 Peter 1:13*—"fix your hope completely on the grace to be brought to you at the revelation of Jesus Christ."

- *Jude 21*—"waiting anxiously for the mercy of our Lord Jesus Christ to eternal life."

- *Revelation 3:11; 22:7,12,20*—"I am coming quickly!"

- *Revelation 22:17,20*—"And the Spirit and the bride say, 'Come.' And let the one who hears say, 'Come.'… He who testifies to these things says, 'Yes, I am coming quickly.' Amen. Come, Lord Jesus."

As we consider the above passages, we note that Christ may come at any moment, that the rapture is actually imminent. Only pretribulationism can give a full, literal meaning to such an any-moment event. Other rapture views must redefine *imminence* more loosely than the New Testament would allow. Dr. Walvoord declares, "The exhortation to look for 'the glorious appearing' of Christ to His own (Titus 2:13) loses its significance if the Tribulation must intervene first. Believers in that case should look for signs."[37] If the pretrib view of imminence is not accepted, then it would make sense to look for signs related to events of the tribulation (i.e., the Antichrist, the two witnesses, etc.) and not for Christ Himself. But the New Testament, as demonstrated above, uniformly instructs the church to look for the coming of Christ, while tribulation saints are told to look for signs.

The New Testament exhortation to be comforted by the Lord's coming (John 14:1-3; 1 Thessalonians 4:18) would no longer have meaning if believers first had to pass through any part of the tribulation. Instead, comfort would have to await passage through the events of the tribulation. No, the church has been given a "blessed hope" in part because our Lord's return is truly imminent.

The early church had a special greeting for one another, as recorded in 1 Corinthians 16:22, which was "Maranatha!" Maranatha consists of three Aramaic words: *Mar* ("Lord"), *ana* ("our"), and *tha* ("come"), meaning "our Lord, come." Such a unique greeting reflects an eager expectation of the blessed hope as a very real presence in the everyday lives these ancient Christians. The life of the church today could only be improved if "Maranatha" were to return as a sincere greeting on the lips of an expectant people. Maranatha!

12. Why is the nature of the tribulation significant?

The Bible teaches that the tribulation (i.e., the seven-year, seventieth week of Daniel) is a time of preparation for Israel's restoration and conversion (Deuteronomy 4:29,30; Jeremiah 30:3-11; Zechariah 12:10).[38] While the church will experience tribulation in general during this present age (John 16:33), she is never mentioned as participating in Israel's time of trouble, which includes the great tribulation, the day of the Lord, and the wrath of God.

Not one Old Testament passage on the tribulation refers to the church (Deuteronomy 4:29,30; Jeremiah 30:4-11; Daniel 8:24-27; 12:1,2), nor does the New Testament ever speak of the church in relation to the tribulation (Matthew 13:30,39-42,48-50; 24:15-31; 1 Thessalonians 1:9,10; 5:4-9; 2 Thessalonians 2:1-11; Revelation 4–18). Such silence speaks loudly and supports the pretrib position.

If pretribulationism is indeed the teaching of Scripture, then we would expect that passages dealing with the tribulation would consistently make no mention of the church. This is exactly what we find. However, Israel is mentioned often throughout these texts. Dr. Robert Gromacki has studied Revelation 4–19, which gives the most detailed overview of the seven-year tribulation in the Bible, and has shown the following:

However, there is a strange silence of the term in chapters 4–19. That fact is especially noteworthy when you contrast that absence with its frequent presence in the first three chapters. One good reason for this phenomenon is the absence of the true church and true evangelical churches in the seven years preceding the Second Coming. The true believers of the church have gone into the presence of Christ in heaven before the onset of the events of the seven year period. The church is not mentioned during the seal, trumpet, and bowl judgments because the church is not here during the outpouring of these judgments.[39]

Only pretribulationism is able to give full import to tribulation terms like "the time of Jacob's distress" (Jeremiah 30:7), as a passage specifically stating that the tribulation is for Jacob (i.e., Israel). Since God's purpose for the tribulation is to restore Israel (Jeremiah 30:3,10) and judge the Gentiles (Jeremiah 30:11), it is clear that this purpose does not include the church. This explains why she will be taken to heaven before this time.

13. Why is the nature of the church significant?

God's plan and purpose for the church would naturally relate to whether He will remove His bride before the tribulation or have her go through it. Only pretribulationism is able to give full biblical import to the New Testament teaching that the church differs significantly from Israel. The church is said to be a mystery (Ephesians 3:1-13) by which Jews and Gentiles are now united into one body in Christ (Ephesians 2:11-22). This explains why the church's translation to heaven is never mentioned in any Old Testament passage that deals with the second coming after the tribulation, and why the church is promised deliverance from the time of God's wrath during the tribulation (1 Thessalonians 1:9,10; 5:9; Revelation 3:10).

It is helpful in determining the timing of the rapture to note that the translation of the church is never mentioned at all in passages that speak of the second coming of Christ after the tribulation.[40] The apostle Paul notes in the following passages that the church is not appointed to God's wrath that will be dispensed during the seven years of the tribulation:

- *Romans 5:9*—"Much more then, having now been justified by His blood, we shall be saved from the wrath of God through Him."

- *1 Thessalonians 1:9,10*—"You turned to God from idols to serve a living and true God, and to wait for His Son from heaven, whom He raised from the dead, that is Jesus, who delivers us from the wrath to come."

- *1 Thessalonians 5:9*—"For God has not destined us for wrath, but for obtaining salvation through our Lord Jesus Christ."

Because God has promised that the church cannot enter the time of "the wrath of the Lamb" or "the great day of their wrath" (Revelation 6:16,17), the church will be taken to heaven before this time.

Forgiveness of sins through Christ prepares the church so that she will not be overtaken by the day of the Lord (1 Thessalonians 5:1-9), which includes the tribulation. This will be accomplished through the rapture, mentioned in the preceding chapter (1 Thessalonians 4:13-18).

Through the church of Philadelphia (Revelation 3:10), the church is explicitly promised deliverance from "the hour of testing," which is the tribulation. Here is a clear passage teaching that the church will escape the tribulation, since God has purposed that it will be "to test those who dwell upon the earth."

- *Revelation 3:10*—" 'Because you have kept the word of My perseverance, I also will keep you from the hour of testing, that hour which is about to come upon the whole world, to test those who dwell upon the earth.' "

Believers are promised deliverance from the *hour* of testing. This means that the church is totally absent from the time period of this hour of testing. It is said to be a worldwide time of testing. Further, it will test "those who dwell upon the earth." The single Greek word for "earth dwellers" is used ten other times in Revelation (6:10; 8:13; 11:10 [twice]; 13:8,12,14 [twice]; 17:2,8) as "a company of people constantly in view through the Apocalypse as objects of God's wrath because of their rebellion against Him. . . . These are men given up to evil and hatred of God's saints."[41] Thus, a contrast between what God has in store for His church and unbelievers could not be greater. Every aspect of this passage supports pretribulationism.

The godly remnant of the tribulation are pictured as Israelites, not members of the church. Thus, pretribulationists do not confuse general terms like *elect* and *saints*, which are used in the Bible of all the saved of the ages, with specific terms like *church* and *those in Christ*, which refer to believers of this age only.

The nature and purpose of the church is said to be unique and separate from Israel. This provides a biblical basis for removal of the church before God completes the final seven years leading up to Israel's redemption. We have seen that there are specific passages promising the church's removal before the time of the tribulation gets under way. This can only make sense with a pretrib understanding.

14. How is the work of the Holy Spirit related to the rapture?

Second Thessalonians 2:1-12 discusses a man of lawlessness being held back until a later time. Interpreting the restrainer of evil (2:6) as the indwelling ministry of the Holy Spirit at work through the body of Christ during the current age supports the pretribulational interpretation. Since "the lawless one" (the beast or Antichrist) cannot be revealed until the restrainer (the Holy Spirit) is taken away (2:7,8), the tribulation cannot occur until the church is removed.

Key to the above scenario is whether the Holy Spirit is the restrainer. After surveying various interpretations of the passage, Dr. Robert Thomas concludes:

> To one familiar with the Lord Jesus' Upper Room Discourse, as Paul undoubtedly was, fluctuation between neuter and masculine recalls how the Holy Spirit is spoken of. Either gender is appropriate, depending on whether the speaker (or writer) thinks of natural agreement (masc. because of the Spirit's personality) or grammatical (neuter because of the noun *pneuma*; see John 14:26; 15:26; 16:13,14).... This identification of the restrainer with deep roots in church history...is most appealing. The special presence of the Spirit as the indweller of saints will terminate abruptly at the *parousia* as it began abruptly at Pentecost. Once the body of Christ has been caught away to heaven, the Spirit's ministry will revert back to what he did for believers during the OT period.... His function of restraining evil through the body of Christ (John 16:7-11; 1 John 4:4) will cease similarly to the way he terminated his striving in the days

of Noah (Genesis 6:3). At that point the reins will be removed from lawlessness and the Satanically inspired rebellion will begin. It appears that *to katechon* ("what is holding back") was well known at Thessalonica as a title for the Holy Spirit on whom the readers had come to depend in their personal attempts to combat lawlessness (1 Thessalonians 1:6; 4:8; 5:19; 2 Thessalonians 2:13).[42]

A natural interpretation of this passage leads to identifying the Holy Spirit as the restrainer. This view supports pretribulationism.

15. Are there other arguments for pretribulationism?

In addition to arguments already presented in this work, there are additional reasons to believe in pretribulationism. These arguments vary in their degree of support of pretribulationism, but should not be overlooked or ignored.

- Our Lord told His disciples of the possibility of believers escaping the tribulation in Luke 21:36: "But keep on the alert at all times, praying in order that you may have strength to escape all these things that are about to take place, and to stand before the Son of Man." It was later revealed through the apostles that such a possibility would indeed become a reality for the church.

- Divine deliverance is a pattern often exercised by God preceding His judgment. This is clearly illustrated in the cases of Enoch, Noah, Lot, Rahab, etc. (2 Peter 2:5-9). For example, when we look at the story of Enoch, we find an illustration of both deliverance and rapture before judgment. Notice the strong emphasis on physical deliverance from judgment as the New Testament in Hebrews 11:5 comments on this Old Testament event:

  > By faith Enoch was taken up so that he should not see death; and he was not found because God took him up; for he obtained the witness that before his being taken up he was pleasing to God.

- God will call His ambassadors home before declaring war on the world, just as in contemporary international relations a nation calls home its ambassador prior to a declaration or act of war. Dr. Ed Hindson notes, "In 2 Corinthians 5:20, believers are called 'Christ's Ambassadors' who appeal to the world to be reconciled to God before it is too late. In biblical times, one's ambassadors were recalled when it was time to make war with the enemy."[43] Such a notion supports only pretribulationism.

- Revelation 4–19 is widely recognized as descriptive of the tribulation. On the other hand, Revelation 2–3 provides instruction relating to the church. The pretrib rapture is reflected in the fact that the apostle John is invited to come up to heaven (Revelation 4:1) at the very point in the biblical text (between Revelation 3 and 4) where pretribulationists say the rapture will occur.

P A R T   4

What Is the Significance of the Pretribulational Rapture for the Believer Today?

16. How does the rapture promote holy living?

Like all aspects of biblical doctrine, teaching on the rapture has a practical dimension. Earlier we noted that the rapture scenario is modeled after the engagement and marriage cycle in ancient Israel. After the engagement, known as a betrothal, which was more binding than modern engagements, the bridegroom was to busy himself with building a room at his father's house so that when the marriage did occur they would have a place to live (John 14:1-3). This interim period, usually at least a year, was viewed as a time of testing the bride's loyalty to see if she would remain chaste and true to the groom. All the while, during the absence, the bride busied herself by preparing her wardrobe and looking forward to the day when she would be united to her beloved. So it is with the church while Christ is absent.

The church is looking for Christ's return at the rapture, as an engaged young girl would anticipate marriage with her beloved: "And though you have not seen Him, you love Him" (1 Peter 1:8). The life each believer lives until Christ's return is a test of loyalty and faithfulness, which is motivated out of a desire to be found pure when He does come for His church.

The rapture is not just wishful "pie-in-the-sky in the by-and-by" thinking. Rather, it is vitally connected to Christian living in the "nasty here-and-now." Any believer with love in his or her heart for the coming Savior will want to live a pure and holy life until His return:

> Beloved, now we are children of God, and it has not appeared as yet what we shall be. We know that, when He appears, we shall be like Him, because we shall see Him just as He is. And everyone who has this hope fixed on Him purifies himself, just as He is pure (1 John 3:2,3).

Note that this passage directly links our present Christian conduct to a future event—the rapture. Why? Because our destiny as God's children is not complete in this life, and it is toward that future goal that we are moving. At the rapture, when we will receive our resurrection bodies, our character will also be perfected. But in the meantime, we are to be purified in present conduct by fixing our hope on the return of Christ. According to this passage, this should be a motivation to holy living.

Many people do not realize how often the New Testament mentions our future blessed hope as a motive for godly living in the present. Note also the following verses:

> Since all these things are to be destroyed in this way, what sort of people ought you to be in holy conduct and godliness, looking for and hastening the coming of the day of God, on account of which the heavens will be destroyed by burning, and the elements will melt with intense heat!... Therefore, beloved, since you look for these things, be diligent to be found by Him in peace, spotless and blameless, and regard the patience of our Lord to be salvation; just as also our beloved brother Paul, according to the wisdom given him, wrote to you (2 Peter 3:11,12,14,15).

In this passage, Peter's admonition refers to the second coming and not to the rapture, but he takes the same approach used by John in that he shows how a future event should impact the present life of a believer. Peter reasons that "holy conduct and godliness" should spring forth from a right contemplation of God's future judgment. Further, Christians are to "Be diligent to be found by Him in peace, spotless and blameless" in this present life. Since Peter calls for "diligence," it is required that a believer put forth a specific effort toward holy living. It does not just happen. We also see an opportunity for salvation during the interim between the Lord's comings.

There are over 20 specific references in the New Testament that link the present conduct of believers to our future destiny. Our rapture hope is said to urge a watchfulness for Christ Himself (1 Corinthians 15:58); to encourage faithfulness in church leaders (2 Timothy 4:1-5); to encourage patient waiting (1 Thessalonians 1:10); to result in expectation and looking (Philippians 3:20; Titus 2:13; Hebrews 9:28); to promote godly moderation (Philippians 4:5); to excite "heavenly mindedness" (Colossians 3:1-4); to bring forth successful labor (1 Thessalonians 2:19,20); to experience comfort (1 Thessalonians 4:18); to urge steadfastness (2 Thessalonians 2:1,2; 1 Timothy 6:14; 1 Peter 5:4); to infuse diligence and activity (2 Timothy 4:1-8); to promote mortification of the flesh (Colossians 3:4,5; Titus 2:12,13); to require soberness (1 Thessalonians 5:6; 1 Peter 1:13); to contribute to an abiding with Christ (1 John 2:28; 3:2); to support patience under trial (James 5:7,8); and to enforce obedience (2 Timothy 4:1).

Dr. Renald Showers summarized some practical implications of the pretrib rapture when he noted:

The imminent coming of Christ should have an incredible practical effect on the lives of individual Christians and the church as a whole. The fact that the glorified, holy Son of God could step through the door of heaven at any moment is intended by God to be the most pressing, incessant motivation for holy living and aggressive ministry (including missions, evangelism, and Bible teaching), and the greatest cure for lethargy and apathy. It should make a major difference in every Christian's values, actions, priorities and goals.[44]

17. How does the rapture promote evangelism?

We noted in Question 16 that 2 Peter 3 teaches that our Lord's return is to be seen by Christians not as a delay, but as an opportunity for those who have not yet trusted Christ to come to faith (2 Peter 3:8,9,14,15). Thus, the imminent coming of Christ at the rapture has often spurred many into an urgent state of evangelistic zeal.

Dr. Tim LaHaye has pointed out that those impacted by a biblical belief in the pretrib rapture often produce "an evangelistic church of soul-winning Christians, for when we believe Christ could appear at any moment, we seek to share Him with our friends lest they be left behind at His coming."[45]

In our own lifetime, we know of many contemporaries who have come to faith in Christ as a result of evangelistic efforts through the vehicle of prophetic preaching. Specifically, hundreds of thousands of Christians have been motivated to give an evangelistic witness as a result of such books as Hal Lindsey's *Late Great Planet Earth*. And thousands of people have come to faith in Christ as a result of the influence of Lindsey's books which focus on the pretrib rapture.

Belief in pretribulationism promotes evangelism when believers are impacted by the fact that Christ could return at any moment, without any prior warning. Thus, a premium is placed upon any and every opportunity to evangelize the lost. Wherever those who believe in an any-moment return of Christ have realized the implications of such a view, it has always provided a powerful motive for evangelism.

18. How does the rapture promote world missions?

If pretribulationism has provoked many to evangelism, then it would also serve as a great stimulus for world missions. Such has been the case.

Dr. LaHaye has noted:

> Belief in the imminent return of Christ impels Christians and churches to develop a worldwide missionary vision of reaching the lost for Christ in this generation. We have more reason to believe that Christ will come in our lifetime than any generation since He ascended into heaven and promised to return. Naturally, we should eagerly desire to reach friends with His good news.[46]

Dr. Timothy Weber, a church historian, has noted that belief in the rapture has been a great incentive for missions in the last 150 years:

> By the 1920s premillennialists were claiming that they made up "an overwhelming majority" of the [missions] movement. Others estimated that believers in the imminent second coming made up from 75 to 85 percent of the missionary force worldwide.... American premillennialists were better represented on the mission fields than in the home churches.... Instead of cutting missionary involvement, premillennialism increased it.[47]

In spite of the fact that some critics say belief in an any-moment return of Christ is a hindrance to missions, reality demonstrates just the opposite to be the case. Belief in pretribulationism has had and will continue to have a positive impact upon the worldwide missionary effort.

Conclusion

The doctrine of the pretribulational rapture offers Christians great hope for the future. The Bible never intends that doctrine and the spiritual life be separated. The study of prophecy and an understanding of the rapture provide us with both a knowledge of the Word of God and a daily hope for the return of Christ as we wait for Him and proclaim His gospel.

Notes

1. Jeffery L. Sheler, "The Christmas Covenant," *U.S. News & World Report*, December 19, 1994, pp. 62, 64.
2. *Dictionary of New Testament Theology*, s.v. "Snatch," by C. Brown, 3:602.
3. Kenneth Gentry, Jr., *He Shall Have Dominion: A Postmillennial Eschatology* (Tyler, TX: Institute for Christian Economics, 1992), pp. 146, 148.
4. *Webster's New Twentieth Century Dictionary*, unabridged, second edition, p. 1055.
5. Paul Lee Tan, *The Interpretation of Prophecy* (Winona Lake, IN: Assurance Publishers, 1974), p. 29.
6. Roy B. Zuck, *Basic Bible Interpretation: A Practical Guide to Discovering Biblical Truth* (Wheaton, IL: Victor Books, 1991), p. 100.
7. Ibid., pp. 100-01.
8. Tan, *Interpretation of Prophecy*, p. 103.

9. Zuck, *Basic Bible Interpretation*, p. 77.

10. David L. Cooper, *The World's Greatest Library: Graphically Illustrated* (Los Angeles: Biblical Research Society, 1970), p. 11.

11. Elliott E. Johnson, *Expository Hermeneutics: An Introduction* (Grand Rapids: Zondervan, 1990), p. 9.

12. Charles C. Ryrie, *Basic Theology: A Popular Systematic Guide to Understanding Biblical Truth* (Wheaton, IL: Victor Books, 1986), p. 450.

13. Arnold Fruchtenbaum, "Israel and the Church" in Wesley Willis, John Master, and Charles Ryrie, eds., *Issues in Dispensationalism* (Chicago: Moody Press, 1994), p. 129.

14. Ibid., p. 113.

15. Ibid., pp. 113-15.

16. Ibid., p. 116.

17. Ibid.

18. Ibid.

19. Ibid., p. 117.

20. Ibid.

21. Ibid.

22. Ibid., pp. 117-18.

23. Ibid., p. 118.

24. Ibid.

25. Ibid., p. 124.

26. Ibid., p. 126.

27. Ibid., p. 118.

28. John S. Feinberg, "Arguing for the Rapture: Who Must Prove What and How" in Thomas Ice and Timothy Demy, eds., *When the Trumpet Sounds* (Eugene, OR: Harvest House Publishers, 1995), p. 194.

29. Edward E. Hindson, "The Rapture and the Return: Two Aspects of Christ's Coming" in Thomas Ice and Timothy Demy, eds., *When the Trumpet Sounds* (Eugene, OR: Harvest House Publishers, 1995), p. 158.

30. The quotation and the first six contrasts in the graphic are taken from John F. Walvoord, *The Return of the Lord* (Grand Rapids: Zondervan, 1955), pp. 87,88.

31. Hindson, "The Rapture and the Return," p. 157.

32. Many of the points in this section are taken from John F. Walvoord, *The Rapture Question: Revised and Enlarged Edition* (Grand Rapids: Zondervan, 1979), pp. 274,75.

33. Charles C. Ryrie, *Revelation* (Chicago: Moody Press, 1968), pp. 35,36.

34. Walvoord, *The Rapture Question*, p. 274.

35. Renald Showers, *Maranatha: Our Lord, Come! A Definitive Study of the Rapture of the Church* (Bellmawr, NJ: The Friends of Israel Gospel Ministry, Inc., 1995), p. 243.

36. Ibid., pp. 127-28.

37. Walvoord, *The Rapture Question*, p. 273.

38. These arguments are adopted from Walvoord, *The Rapture Question*, pp. 270-71.

39. Robert Gromacki, "Where is 'The Church' in Revelation 4–19?" in Thomas Ice and Timothy Demy, eds., *When the Trumpet Sounds* (Eugene, OR: Harvest House Publishers, 1995), p. 355.

40. These arguments are adopted from Walvoord, *The Rapture Question*, pp. 271-73.

41. Robert L. Thomas, *Revelation 1–7: An Exegetical Commentary* (Chicago: Moody Press, 1992), p. 289.

42. Robert L. Thomas, "2 Thessalonians," in *The Expositor's Bible Commentary*, vol. 11, Frank E. Gaebelein, ed. (Grand Rapids: Zondervan, 1978), pp. 324-25.

43. Hindson, "The Rapture and the Return," p. 161.

44. Showers, *Maranatha*, pp. 255-56.

45. Tim LaHaye, *No Fear of the Storm* (Portland, OR: Multnomah Press, 1992), p. 18.

46. LaHaye, *No Fear*, p. 18.

47. Timothy P. Weber, *Living in the Shadow of the Second Coming: American Premillennialism, 1875-1982* (Grand Rapids: Zondervan, 1983), p. 81.

Recommended Reading

Beechick, Allen. *The Pre-Tribulation Rapture*. Denver: Accent Books, 1980.

Blackstone, William E. *Jesus Is Coming*. New York: Revell, 1898, 1908, 1932.

Boyer, James L. *Prophecy: Things to Come*. Winona Lake, IN: B.M.H. Books, 1973.

Brookes, James H. *Maranatha*. New York: Fleming H. Revell Company, 1889.

_____. *Till He Come*. New York: Fleming H. Revell Company, 1895.

Darby, J.N. *Will the Saints Be in the Tribulation?* New York: Loizeaux Brothers, n.d.

Duty, Guy. *Escape from the Coming Tribulation*. Minneapolis: Bethany Fellowship, 1975.

English, E. Schuyler. *Re-Thinking the Rapture*. Neptune, NJ: Loizeaux Brothers, 1954.

* Feinberg, Paul D. "The Case for the Pretribulation Rapture Position" in Richard R. Reiter, Paul D. Feiberg, Gleason L. Archer, Douglas J. Moo, *The Rapture: Pre-, Mid-, or Post-Tribulational?* Grand Rapids: Zondervan, 1984.

* Fruchtenbaum, Arnold G. *The Footsteps of the Messiah: A Study of the Sequence of Prophetic Events*. Tustin, CA: Ariel Ministries, 1982.

Harrison, William K. *Hope Triumphant: The Rapture of the Church*. Chicago: Moody Press, 1966.

Hoyt, Herman A. *The End Times*. Chicago: Moody Press, 1969.

* Ice, Thomas and Demy, Timothy, eds., *When the Trumpet Sounds: Today's Foremost Authorities Speak Out on End-Time Controversies*. Eugene, OR: Harvest House Publishers, 1995.

Ironside, H.A. *Not Wrath, But Rapture*. New York: Loizeaux Brothers, 1946.

* LaHaye, Timothy. *No Fear of the Storm: Why Christians Will Escape All the Tribulation*. Portland: Multnomah Press, 1992.

Lindsey, Hal. *The Rapture: Truth or Consequences*. New York: Bantam Books, 1983.

Mayhue, Richard L. *Snatched Before the Storm? A Case for Pretribulationism*. Winona Lake, IN: BMH Books, 1980.

Pache, René. *The Return of Jesus Christ.* Chicago: Moody Press, 1955, 1975.

Pentecost, J. Dwight. *Things to Come: A Study in Biblical Eschatology.* Grand Rapids: Zondervan Publishing House, 1958.

Ryrie, Charles C. *What You Should Know About the Rapture.* Chicago: Moody Press, 1981.

Scofield, C. I. *Will the Church Pass Through the Great Tribulation?* Philadelphia: Philadelphia School of the Bible, 1917.

* Showers, Renald. *Maranatha: Our Lord, Come!* Bellmawr, NJ: The Friends of Israel Gospel Ministry, 1995.

* Stanton, Gerald B. *Kept from the Hour: Biblical Evidence for the Pretribulational Return of Christ,* fourth edition. Miami Springs, FL: Schoettle Publishing Co., [1956], 1991.

Strombeck, J. F. *First the Rapture.* Eugene, OR.: Harvest House Publishers, [1950] 1982.

Thiessen, Henry C. *Will the Church Pass Through the Tribulation?* New York: Loizeaux Brothers, 1941.

* Walvoord, John F. *The Blessed Hope and the Tribulation.* Grand Rapids: Zondervan, 1976.

* _____. *The Rapture Question.* Grand Rapids: Zondervan, [1957], 1979.

_____. *The Return of the Lord.* Grand Rapids: Zondervan, 1955.

_____. *Major Bible Prophecies: 37 Crucial Prophecies That Affect You Today.* Grand Rapids: Zondervan, 1991.

_____. *Prophecy: 14 Essential Keys to Understanding the Final Drama.* Nashville: Thomas Nelson Publishers, 1993.

Wood, Leon. *Is The Rapture Next?* Grand Rapids: Zondervan, 1956.

(*) highly recommended